Animal Names In Hindi For E

Sourav Rana

Published By Sourav Rana At

Amazon

Copyright 2020 Sourav Rana

Amazon Edition License Notes
Thank you for downloading this eBook. This eBook remains the copyrighted property of the author. This book may not be reproduced, copied and distributed for commercial as well as non-commercial purposes. If you enjoyed this book, please return to your favorite eBook retailer to discover other works by this author. Thank you for your support.

PREFACE

Hindi is one of the most spoken languages in the world. It is also the prominent language of India. It is spoken by around 300 million people. It has also received the status of the official language of India. Here I will give you the knowledge of different animals name in Hindi language. Originally the Hindi is written in Devanagari script but the Hindi names in this book have been provided in roman script for the ease of understanding of English readers

I hope that you will like this edition. If you have any questions, concerns or feedback please feel free to reach me through at iwriter.sourav@gmail.com

Thanks for taking time to read.

Author

The animals play a very important role in our lives. We have been dependent on these loyal and gullible creatures for many things essential for our daily lives. To list a few of these things are milk, clothes, fur and medicines etc. Since the dawn of human civilization, they have stood shoulder to shoulder with human beings on the path of evolution. Animal importance can be found in religious literature and epics all around the world. In many cultures, there are the rituals of worshipping them like the gods. The thing that is important for the human being will definitely find a name in their languages. The animals have been given different names in different languages. Today we will discuss the names given for 50 different animals in one of such language which is the Hindi. Let us start our task now.

Animal Names In Hindi:-

1. Cow

In Hindi, the Cow is called "Guy". Also, it is one of the most sacred animals in the Hindu religion(the largest religious faith in India).

Cow|Guy

Sentence Usage

English Sentence:- Cow's milk is considered to be very useful in India.

Hindi Translation:- Bharat main Guy ka doodh bahut laabhdayak maana jaata hai.

2. Bull

The Hindi name for Bull is "Bel". The Hindu God Shiva is depicted riding a bull in pictures and sculptures.

Bull | Bel

Sentence Usage

English Sentence:- The bull had not observed her.

Hindi translation:- Bel ne usey dekha nahi tha.

3. Buffalo

The Buffalo is called "Bhains" in Hindi.

Buffalo/Bhains

Sentence Usage

English Sentence:- It took us two hour to locate the buffalo.

Hindi translation:- Hamein Bhains dhoondhne mein dow ghante lag gye.

4. Camel

The Hindi name for Camel is "Oont".

Camel/Oont

Sentence Usage

English Sentence:- The camel has a hump on its back.

Hindi translation:- Oont ki peeth par ek koobar hota hai.

5. Dog

The Dog is called "Kutta" in Hindi.

Dog/Kutta

Sentence Usage

English sentence:- My dog is very loyal to me.

Hindi translation:- Mera Kutta mere prati bahot wafaadaar hai.

6. Bitch

The Hindi name for Bitch is "Kutiya".

Bitch|Kutiya

Sentence Usage

English Sentence:- They have a black bitch.

Hindi translation:- Unke paas ek kaali Kutiya hai.

7. Lion

The Lion is called "Sher" in Hindi.

Lion/Sher

Sentence Usage

English Sentence:- The lion is the king of forest.

Hindi translation:- Sher jungle kaa raja hai.

8. Lioness

The Hindi name for Lioness is "Sherni".

Lioness / Sherni

Sentence Usage

English Sentence:- The lioness was fighting to protect her cubs.

Hindi translation:- Sherni apne shavakon ko bachaane ke liye lar rahi thi.

9. Bear

The Bear is called "Bhaalu" in Hindi.

Bear/Bhaalu

Sentence Usage

English Sentence:- The bear can climb trees.

Hindi translation:- Bhaalu perron par char sakta hai.

10. Monkey

The Hindi name for Monkey is "Bandar".

Monkey/Bandar

Sentence Usage

English Sentence:- The monkey fell from the tree.

Hindi translation:- Bandar per se gir geya.

11. Elephant

The elephant is called "Haathee" in Hindi.

Elephant/Haathee

Sentence Usage

English Sentence:- An elephant hulked up suddenly before us.

Hindi translation:- Ek Haathee achaanak hamaare saamne aa gya.

12. Deer

The deer is called "Hiran" in Hindi.

Deer|Hiran

Sentence Usage

English sentence:- They were trailing a deer.

Hindi translation:- Ve ek Hiran ka peechha kar rahe they.

13. Doe

The Hindi name of doe is "Hiranee".

Sentence Usage

English Sentence:- We saw a doe in the zoo.

Hindi translation:- Hamne chiriyaghar me ek Hiranee dekhi.

14. Stag

The Hindi name for stag is "Barasingha".

Stag/Barasingha

Sentence Usage

English Sentence:- The stag is a rare animal species.

Hindi Translation:- Barasingha ek durlabh prajaati ka jaanver hai.

15. Pig

The pig is called "Sooyar" in Hindi. Also the Hindi name of wild pig is "Jungli Sooyar".

Pig/Sooyar

Sentence Usage

English Sentence:- They have a pig farm.

Hindi Translation:- Unke paas ek Sooyar paalan kender hai.

16. Snake

The Hindi name for snake is "Saamp".

Snake/Saamp

Sentence Usage

English Sentence:- She screamed when she saw the snake.

Hindi Translation:- Jab usne Saamp dekha tab vo chillaayi.

17. Tiger

The tiger is called "Baagh" in Hindi.

Tiger | Baagh

Sentence Usage

English Sentence:- She gave me a picture of tiger.

Hindi Translation:- Usne mujhe Baagh ki ek tasveer dee.

18. Turtle

The Hindi name for turtle is "Kachhuyaa".

Turtle/Kachhuyaa

Sentence Usage

English Sentence:- The turtle moves very slowly.

Hindi Translation:- Kachhuyaa bahut dhime se chalta hai.

19. Sheep

The sheep is called "Bher" in Hindi.

Sheep / Bher

Sentence Usage

English Sentence:- We get wool from the sheep.

Hindi Translation:- Bher se hamein oon praapat hoti hai.

20. Cat

The Hindi name for cat is "Billi".

Cat / Billi

Sentence Usage

English Sentence:- They found the cat up on the roof

Hindi Translation:- Unhe Billi shat ke uper milli.

21. Mouse

The mouse is called "Choohaa" in Hindi.

Mouse | Choohaa

Sentence Usage

English Sentence:- The mouse is a small animal.

Hindi Translation:- Choohaa ek shotaa jaanver hai.

22. Rabbit

The rabbit is called "Khargosh" in Hindi.

Rabbit/Khargosh

Sentence Usage

English Sentence:- The rabbit disappeared in the woods.

Hindi Translation:- Khargosh jungle mein gayab ho gya.

23. Fish

The Hindi name for fish is "Mashli".

Fish/Mashli

Sentence Usage

English Sentence:- The best fish swims near the bottom of the pond.

Hindi Translation:- Sabse behtreen Mashli taalaab ke tal par tairti hai.

24. Horse

The horse is called "Ghora" in Hindi.

Horse/Ghora

Sentence Usage

English Sentence:- They have a white horse.

Hindi Translation:- Unke paas ek safed Ghora hai.

25. Goat

The Hindi name for goat is "Bakri".

Goat/Bakri

Sentence Usage

English Sentence:- The goat's milk is very hygienic.

Hindi Translation:- Bakri kaa doodh bahut swasthyakar hota hai.

26. Fox

The fox is called "Lomri" in Hindi.

Fox/Lomri

Sentence Usage

English Sentence:- The fox was chasing a rabbit.

Hindi Translation:- Lomri ek khargosh kaa peecha kar rahi thi.

27. Butterfly

The Hindi name for butterfly is "Titli".

Butterfly/Titli

Sentence Usage

English Sentence:- The blue colour butterfly was looking very beautiful.

Hindi Translation:- Neele rang ki Titli bahut sunder lag rahi thi.

28. Frog

The Hindi name for frog is "Mendak".

Frog/Mendak

Sentence Usage

English Sentence:- She screamed when she saw the frog coming towards herself.

Hindi Translation:- Jab usne Mendak ko apni taraf aatey dekha tab vo chillaayi.

29. Bat

The bat is called "Chamgaadar" in Hindi.

Bat / Chamgaadar

Sentence Usage

English Sentence:- The bat was flying with swiftness.

Hindi Translation:- Chamgaadar tejee se ud rahi thi.

30. Spider

The Hindi name for spider is "Makri".

Spider/Makri

Sentence Usage

English Sentence:- I saw a spider walking on the ceiling.

Hindi Translation:- Maine ek Makri ko shat per chalte dekha.

31. Squirrel

The Hindi name for squirrel is "Gilehari".

Squirrel/Gilehari

Sentence Usage

English Sentence:- The squirrel was eating almonds.

Hindi Translation:- Gilehari badam kha rahi thee.

32. Leopard

The leopard is called "Tenduya" in Hindi.

Leopard/Tenduya

Sentence Usage

English Sentence:- The city was put on high alert after the sighting of a wild leopard was reported.

Hindi Translation:- Ek jungli Tenduya dekhe jaane ki soochna milne ke baad sheher ko uch starkata par rakhaa gya thaa.

33. Lizard

The lizard is called "Shipkali" in Hindi.

Lizard/Shipkali

Sentence Usage

English Sentence:- The lizard got close to the bulb.

Hindi Translation:- Shipkali bulb ke paas pahunch gyi.

34. Chameleon

The Hindi name for chameleon is "Girgit".

Chameleon|Girgit

Sentence Usage

English Sentence:- Chameleon can change its color.

Hindi Translation:- Girgit apna rang badal sakta hai.

35. Wolf

The Hindi name for wolf is "Bheriya".

Wolf/Bheriya

Sentence Usage

English Sentence:- It's a wolf! I'm sure.

Hindi Translation:- Ye ek Bheriya hai muje poora yakeen hai.

36. Crocodile

The crocodile is called "Magarmachh" in Hindi.

Crocodile|Magarmachh

Sentence Usage

English Sentence:- The crocodile's jaw is very powerful.

Hindi Translation:- Magarmachh ka jabraa bahut shaktishaali hota hai.

37. Hyna

The Hindi name for hyna is "Lakarbaghaa".

Hyna/Lakarbaghaa

Sentence Usage

English Sentence:- The hyna was just behind the bushes.

Hindi Translation:- Lakarbaghaa theek jhaariyon ke peeche thaa.

38. Rhinoceros

The rhinoceros is called "Gendaa" in Hindi.

Rhinoceros | Gendaa

Sentence Usage

English Sentence:- The rhinoceros is very heavy animal.

Hindi Translation:- Gendaa bahut bhaari jaanver hai.

39. Scorpion

The Hindi name for scorpion is "Bichhu".

Scorpion/Bichhu

Sentence Usage

English Sentence:- The scorpion bite is very painful.

Hindi Translation:- Bichhu dansh bahut peeradayak hota hai.

40. Crab

The crab is called "Kekraa" in Hindi.

Crab | Kekraa

Sentence Usage

English Sentence:- I asked him if the crab is an extinct animal species?

Hindi Translation:- Maine usse puchha ki kya Kekra ek durlabh prajaati kaa jaanver hai?

41. Porcupine

The porcupine is called "Saahi" in Hindi.

Porcupine/Saahi

Sentence Usage

English Sentence:- Porcupine can throw spines on a potential threat chasing it.

Hindi Translation:- Sambhaavit khatra apni aur aate dekh Saahi apni peeth par lage kaante phenk sakti hai.

42. Baboon

The Hindi name for baboon is "Langoor".

Baboon/Langoor

Sentence Usage

English Sentence:- It is quite difficult to catch a baboon in the forest.

Hindi Translation:- Jungle mein ek Langoor ko pakar pana kafi mushkil hai.

43. Python

The python is called "Ajgar" in Hindi.

Python / Ajgar

Sentence Usage

English Sentence:- Python is the largest snake found on earth.

Hindi Translation:- Ajgar dharti par paya jaane vaala sabse baraa saamp hai.

44. Monitor lizard

The Hindi name for monitor lizard is "Goh".

Monitor Lizard/Goh

Sentence Usage

English Sentence:- Among reptiles, the monitor lizard is reported to be the prominent.

Hindi Translation:- Srisrapon mein se Goh sabse pramukh maani jati hai.

45. Jackal

The jackal is called "Siyaar" in Hindi.

Jackal/Siyaar

Sentence Usage

English Sentence:- The study was carried out on a jackal for five weeks.

Hindi Translation:- Ek Siyaar par paanch hafton ke liye adhayan kiya gya tha.

46. Mongoose

The Hindi name for mongoose is "Nevlaa".

Mongoose/Nevla

Sentence Usage

English Sentence:- I remember a white-tailed mongoose passed by the fence.

Hindi Translation:- Mujhe yaad hai ki ek safed poonsh wala Nevla baar ke paas se gujra.

47. Earthworm

The earthworm is called "Kenchooya" in Hindi.

Earthworm/Kenchooya

Sentence Usage

English Sentence:- There was an earthworm.

Hindi Translation:- Wahaan ek Kenchooya tha.

48. Beaver

The beaver is called "Udbilaav" in Hindi.

Beaver/Udbilaav

Sentence Usage

English Sentence:- We saw a beaver near the pond.

Hindi Translation:- Hamne talab ke paas ek Udbilaav dekha.

49. Lynx

The Hindi name for lynx is "Banbilaao".

Lynx/Banbilaao

Sentence Usage

English Sentence:- Lynx is the national animal of Romania.

Hindi Translation:- Banbilaao Romania ka raashtriya pashu hai.

50. Bison

The bison is called "Jungli Saand" in Hindi.

Bison / Jungli Saand

Sentence Usage

English Sentence:- The bison was grazing.

Hindi Translation:- Jungli Saand charaayi kar raha tha.

CPSIA information can be obtained
at www.ICGtesting.com
Printed in the USA
BVHW021009280822
645711BV00002B/13